Customer Service

"It's A Life Thing"

Luther T. Collins

Customer Service "It's A Life Thing"

Luther T. Collins

Printed in the United States of America by
Ingram Spark
www.ingramspark.com

Cover design by Vince White
Book Sizing & Binder by Chris Kitt Jr.

ISBN: 978-1-0878-6809-7

To contact author for booking or ordering
additional copies, go to:
luthertcollins0408@gmail.com

Intro

This book was written to give you strategies and wisdom concerning the importance of customer service. This book is a guideline how one should execute, expect, and experience customer service. No longer will you contain customer service to an establishment but you will see it for what it truly is, a lifestyle and way of living. Once we understand the value of customer service than we can truly be successful in living our best lives while being responsible and productive citizens. This book was inspired by the need for the world to overcome this ignorance of not understanding that this is not just a service but a worldwide necessity for survival.

This book should change your perspective on how you give and receive service. There is a saying you never get a second chance to make a first impression. If your initial customer service interaction is bad there may not be a second opportunity.

With everything going on presently in the world today customer service is more critical now than ever before.

Table of Contents

Chapter 1 – What Is Customer Service

Before you can begin to understand how customer service works you must first know what it is. If someone said to you, what is customer service? How would you define it? What would your answer be? First in order to arrive at a definition you must break down each root. Webster defines customer as one that purchases a commodity or service: an individual usually having some specified distinctive trait. Webster defines the word service as a contribution to the welfare of others, a disposal for use, or a help, use, or benefit. While Webster provides some pretty good distinction of customers and service broken down let's dissect them even more and go even further.

So if you ask yourself who is a customer? The answer should be everyone. Any individual and every individual is a customer, no exception. The word customer should be translated into the word guest. How would you treat a guest if they were staying at your house? For most people the natural answer is make them feel at home. A guest should always be shown hospitality and accommodated meaning you take care of a guest. A guest should be obliged and shown companionship. Some other words for guest are visitor, patron, mate, helper, peer, classmate, coworker, bride, sidekick, acquaintance, spouse, friend, colleague, schoolmate, and companion. This just goes to show that a customer is not just an affiliate but a personal encounter. When you understand who a customer consists of it allows you the opportunity to better service their needs. A customer exchange happens unknowingly at the most opportune times. If you make a habit of treating everyone as a customer than you will make everyone's experience enjoyable.

Next you ask what is a service? The answer should be any and every way you respond or interact with an individual. An action directly connected with a customer is another form of what a service is. A service is not always providing a good but a service can simply be an exchange of words or kind gesture. Yes that's correct you can very well service someone with your words as well as deeds. For example opening a door for an elderly person is a service, fixing dinner plates at dinner time is a service, and helping someone up stairs is a service. Another example of a service could be complimenting someone on their outfit or personal appearance. The impact of service is life changing, ever-lasting, and impactful if presented properly.

Customer service leaves a lasting impression with your guest based on your most recent encounter. This basically means how that individual feels about the service you provided or failed to provide is customer service. Based on this encounter the individual will make a decision whether they will come back to you or not for additional interactions. If the customer's needs were not met and your obligation was not fulfilled they will look to go elsewhere when the time comes. While this is easily related to a business remember customer service is a life thing. Although we often limit the sphere of customer service if we made this our daily norm the world we see, love, and experience would be a much better place.

Customer service as it relates to family, friends, or from a personal standpoint will muster the same results. If your interaction or approach is genuine, then the outcome will almost always produce desired results. Customer service has to be a way of living and not a random approach. A lot of times individuals will say I'll treat you right if you treat me right. As a human being it's our responsibility to treat everyone right. Even when others treat you wrong it's still a good practice to treat them right. You never know when you may need that individual or vice versa. It's a saying that says you never bite the hand that feeds you and you never burn your bridges. With that being said you also must use wisdom if someone purposely mistreats you, don't continue giving them new opportunities. Simply saying you choose who you hang around and who resides in your circle. If you allow anyone in your circle who does not value you, then you have the wrong people in your sphere.

Customer Service is a part of everyday life whether you know it or not. People service you through association, affiliation, involvement, dialogue, correspondence, communication, and exchanges as well as interactions or encounters. However on the same spectrum you service people through your actions and reactions. So just focusing on your interactions, would be saying you gave poor or positive customer service? Always ask yourself what can you do differently on the next go round? You should always be looking to improve as it relates to customer service. Focus on yourself and be a leader in customer service. You can't make someone change their service but you can lead by example by being a change agent for others to follow. Never get to a point where you think you have arrived. When you reach this point you no longer have the ability to learn or improve.

If you were to google the word customer service you would see that it refers to a company. While customer service does apply to companies it should never be limited to a company. The definition google gives for customer service is the assistance and advice provided by a company to those people who buy or use its products or services. It also states that customer service is the provision of service to customers before, during, and after a purchase. While customer service is essential to business success it is also a life necessity. If you only apply customer service as it relates to business than you will never truly see its full potential.

Customer service is always two sided regardless of what you previously thought. You as a customer also share the same obligation to service the servicer or the one providing the service. If someone gives you great service, you service that individual by thanking them and showing appreciation. The greatest way to show gratitude as it relates food service is by tipping your waiter or waitress if you are in an establishment. Never shortchange a great experience by not fulfilling your obligation to serve the one who serves you. If you receive amazing service you should always leave an amazing tip. If you can't tip your waiter or waitress, don't dine in. Your dedication in servicing the servicer will ignite and inspire your server to perform at an even greater level. For example if you take Michael Jordan who is often referred to as the Goat (Greatest of All Time) in basketball, in the finals he had some of his best performances by leading his team. He serviced his team by leading them to a championship and playing at the highest level above all others. His team serviced him by acknowledging his craft with fist bumps and celebrations on big and small performances. If MJ's teammates never shared his excitement and acknowledged his talents he would have not experienced the same success. Even cheerleaders need someone to cheer them on because without the crowd, what is a good cheer?

If you fail to service the servicer than you can be responsible for receiving a poor performance or missed assignment. It's never just about you in this life as that is just outright selfishness at its best and will get you nowhere. As a parent it's your responsibility to root for or service your child or children. If you don't believe in your child or children, who will? As a doctor it's your responsibility to cheer on your patients because if you don't believe in them who will as you may be all they have. As a lawyer you are in charge of fighting for your clients for you may be their last lifeline. As a restaurant owner you are responsible for exceeding your guest expectations and ensuring they have an extravagant experience. The greater your title the greater your responsibility to service becomes. If you're an influencer or motivator your assignment of service is not local but global.

When you know and understand what customer service is than you begin to realize its true value and importance. The society we live in today is in definite need of customer service on all levels. Nobody is excluded and everyone is included. There is an urgent need for customer service at your local grocery with the bagger just like there is an urgent need for customer service in the white house with our commander in chief. One bad experience should not discourage you or push you away but it should catapult you to be a service change agent. The goal should never be to focus on the service you don't receive but to be the example of the service you desire to receive.

Nobody is perfect as everyone will fall short and make mistakes. With that being said never let this be the reason you fail to give great life service. What if your service was the difference between life and death? What verdict would be left on your hands? Although it is often over looked and frequently under booked your life service matters. If someone is having a bad day and they run into you, what kind of life service would you leave them with? After meeting you are they ready to commit suicide or hit the reset button? See we never take the time to look at the after effects of our encounters. Although you may never see this individual again you know if you gave them you're best or not. It's like taking a test in school; it's a process just like life. First you are taught the assignment in class, then you review, and next you take the test. First you experience an encounter, then an exchange takes place, and next you exit in hopefully the spirit of excellence.

For those who are unaware a greeting or salutation is a great form of customer service. It doesn't cost you anything to say hello, hi, good morning, good afternoon, good evening, how are you, etc. Not only is it a service to be the greeter but it's also a service to give a return greeting as a greetee. It's never ok not to greet someone who first greets you. You don't have to carry on a conversation but it is common courtesy to greet your neighbor. Never let a title, ethnicity, differences, status, or a pay grade separate you from giving or returning a simple greeting. Remember everyone is human and we were all created equal no matter what accolades we may have. Everybody who has the perception that they are somebody; you were once nobody and should never overlook anybody. Simply spoken don't be rude but be grateful you woke up this morning by greeting your neighbor. Steve Harvey once said, "You will only be remembered by the dash on your tombstone." This simply means one day we will all die and you will be remembered by what you did in your life. So all the accomplishments and accolades will be left behind and all that will remain is memories. Will there be good or bad memories of customer service that carry's on your legacy of life when your time runs out?

Customer Service is the exchange of an encounter between two or more people. The goal should always be to exceed expectations by going above and beyond in every experience. There are different levels of customer service that exist – good, bad, and excellent. Good customer service exists when you do just enough to make a guest happy. Bad customer service is a reflection of poor communication, very little or no effort put forth, and lazy body language. Excellent customer service happens when you build a relationship with the guest and remove I from the equation. When a guest receives excellent customer service they will not only return but tell others of their experience as it's contagious and addictive. You should never ever be content with leaving anything less than your best behind as it relates to customer service and life.

Chapter 2 – It's Bigger Than a Place

Customer service is bigger than a place and must not be put in a box. You can not contain customer service or minimize it. When you shrink customer service, then you eliminate the wow factor. The wow factor is an opportunity to exceed ones expectation as it relates to service. The reason this is so important is because the same way you want someone to go above and beyond for you is the same service your customers want. In fact customer service should always be magnified as it's a big deal. No opportunity is ever too small to make a big impact. If customer service is not an important factor to you, then you are on the wrong side of the fence. You can't just say I want to be the recipient of great customer service if you are not willing to give the same as this is a double standard. A good way of looking at it is never expect something you aren't willing to give.

Let's go a step further a box that's taped closed and sealed good is considered full. So let's just say the box has reached its maximum capacity and nothing else can fit in the box. However if you have more items needing to go in the box but have no space, then you have no where to put the overflow. What if this is the only box you have than those excess items will be wasted due to not having enough space? So we just lost some good merchandise due to lack of space.

Now when we tie this box in to customer service we say I got this much space that I am willing to fill. Let's change the word space into service and change the word fill into give. Now we say I got this much service that I am willing to give. Unknowingly you just placed a cap on the extent of your willingness to provide service. When you put a cap on customer service you are simply saying I will take care of you if it doesn't exceed this limit. For those working directly in the customer service field this should be unacceptable. That's equivalent to having a server and they tell you that you exceeded the limit on free refills. How do you exceed a limit of free refills when you are paying for a service? The answer is simple, by placing a cap on the service you are willing to give. Going back to the box scenario, you should always keep your box open so you can always continue filling your box. The trick is to empty your box by giving all you have on each encounter. The box will overflow at times but your service should also be in the overflow. If your box is always excessively filled up and never emptied out you have to ask yourself if you are really providing good service.

The biggest mistake we make in regards to customer service is placing it in a building. Customer service does not just happen in an establishment but everywhere. Stop limiting customer service to a place; it's much bigger than that. When you put customer service in a box you limit the impact of service. Without a customer or a service being provided there is no customer service.

It never said anything about a location or edifice being necessary. There is nothing that says customer service only applies to someone in a building. When you remove the walls of service, then you open up endless opportunities to be excessive in service.

Say you're driving and a car is trying to get in front of you on a busy intersection. This is probably something you experience frequently but the question is do you let the car in or speed up to keep them from getting in front of you? This particular encounter is not something that takes place in a box, building, or establishment but yet it's an example of customer service. You must ask yourself is it that serious that you have to speed up to keep someone from getting in front of you? This person may be saving you from an accident as nothing ever happens by chance. The sad part is there are probably more individuals who would speed up than allow a car to get in front of them.

Stop putting customer service inside of four walls and start allowing it to do what it was created to do, flourish. Customer service is like a flower, if you water it and feed it you allow it to grow into a thing of beauty. On the other hand if you don't water and feed the flower it dies. If you water and feed customer service it grows. Building a relationship is another word for watering and feeding customer service. On the other side of this if you don't invest in customer service it dies or kills the relationship. Just be mindful the customers you fail to acknowledge or service are the customers who you will no longer see.

Now let's look at customer service in our very own personal lives. If you are on a date do you want your man or woman to extend customer service to you? Let's see how this looks from a real life scenario. Say Roger and Jackie (two fictional characters) have been talking for some time and decide to go on their first date. First to get to this point there was a lot of positive (customer) service that had to take place to get here. One they had to be compatible meaning they have similar interests and are attracted to one another. Two they had to be relatable meaning they can identify with one another and share common ground. Three they had to service each other to get to this point. Servicing from a relationship means giving compliments, kind gestures, gifts, open acknowledgements, honesty, and etc. After we established the need for a joint service exchange between Roger and Jackie we are able to move forward in the dating process. Jackie is excited because Roger has serviced her and Roger is excited because Jackie has serviced him. In a relationship the man should always be the first to give good service.

When Roger arrives to pick up Jackie he compliments her and holds her hand as she walks down the steps. Great service has just taken place in the compliment to build her up and holding of hands walking down the steps just to ensure her safety. Jackie should compliment him back and say thank you as this is her way of servicing him. When they get to the car, Roger opens the door for Jackie as another service and waits for her to get in and settled before closing the door. Jackie again services Roger by saying thank you.

While riding to the restaurant they engage in conversation. The conversation is where the relationship building takes place which consists of fact finding (likes, dislikes, how was your day), compliments (awesome job on getting that promotion at work) as there should never be a shortage of these in any point in any relationship, and background (you should want to know everything about someone you choose to share your world with). They get to the restaurant and again Roger opens the door of the car, holds her hand, and then opens the door of the restaurant. Holding hands can be a form of service as well as it represents safety, security, and sharing (meaning I have something great that I won't ever let go).

Upon entering the restaurant Roger pulls out the chair for Jackie again extending to her the ultimate service. And in exchange Jackie shares her generosity by extending a warm thank you and genuine smiles. At the table they exchange service in the form of conversation until the food arrives. They service each other during the meal by the way they eat and body language. You don't want to be on a date with a messy eater who spills food and drink everywhere as this is poor service. You also don't want a date that reclines in a wooden chair or puts his feet on the table as this is poor body language or service. And you may not enjoy your conversation too much if someone is talking with a mouth full of food. After eating Roger asks for the bill as this again is service (he is treating Jackie to a meal). There is nothing written in stone here but a man should always be willing to treat a woman first as this is just great service and life practice. If you can't service your woman, than another man will. Leaving the restaurant Roger grabs Jackie's hand and pulls her chair back as she gets up from the table and Jackie says thank you. Roger opens all doors and helps Jackie into the car.

They engage in conversation on the way back to Jackie's house. When they arrive to the house Roger opens the door, grabs Jackie's hand, and escorts her up the stairs to her door. Jackie says thank you and Roger says your welcome, kisses Jackie on the cheek and says thank you for an awesome night before returning to the car. You notice Roger does not ask to come in and only kisses her on the cheek. When you truly care about someone you service them by letting them know you are worth waiting for and show them with your actions that they are more than a just a booty call or sexual encounter.

Now if you had to critique Roger's customer service to Jackie what grade would you give him? As you can see this date was not confined to four walls. This is an example of not trying to contain customer service to four walls. If Roger only serviced Jackie when they were only confined to four walls what would have been the impact? This goes to show customer service should never be placed in a box and it's in everything you do. No encounter or interaction should be left void without a great service experience. Because of Roger's service he and Jackie got married later on down the road and had a beautiful family together.

If you noticed we didn't talk about the servers, host or hostess, valet parkers, greeters, or other specific customer service agents. They were all there as they would have had a great impact on the experience if Roger and Jackie were to consider coming back. But our focus was on the date and the customer service exchanged between the two. While it was Roger's responsibility to lead with great customer service it was also Jackie's responsibility to respond with great customer service. And because of the exchange of great service they now have something to build upon. And because of the consistency, genuineness, and realness their kids have now picked up the service torch and ran with it in excellence.

Stop thinking that customer service only takes place in a service specific environment. If you only see customer service as a restaurant experience you will never enjoy the full effects that it can have on your life. Customer service placed in four walls is like placing a dog in a cage. If you confine the service than you never get to enjoy the experience. If you keep the puppy confined you never get to enjoy his company.

Let's go a step further and draw a small box, the dimensions of the box will be four by four by four by four. Now in this box I want you to write everything you want to receive as a customer. Keep in mind you can only write within the four walls of this box. Anything you don't write or can't fit your unable to receive. If this was the case as it relates to customer service you would never experience the best customer service has to offer. It's like going to an amusement park and riding all the new rides. Customer service should always be an enjoyable experience and explosive encounter. This simply means that you had a great time, marvelous memories were made, the limits were removed, the excitement could not be contained, and you can't wait to do it again. This is what great customer service looks like when you erase the boundaries of the box.

Chapter 3 – Everything You Do Is a Service

Customer service does not always come in the form of words. In fact many gestures can be a symbol of customer service. Excusing yourself from the table when you have to burp, fart, blow your nose, or cough can be a form of customer service. Washing your hands when you leave out of a public restroom can be a form of customer service. Ask yourself do you want someone fixing your food that didn't wash their hands coming out of a bathroom stall? What about shaking hands with someone who didn't wash their hands coming directly out of a stall? We don't think about things like this but it happens every day. There is an old saying that says, "Treat others how you want to be treated." It's simple if you don't want someone doing it to you than you don't do it to them. Customer service is not always what you say but it's what you do and don't do. Such as opening a door or carrying a bag for someone. If you see an individual in need and you don't help them you are doing them a disservice. What if it was your mother or grandmother, how would you react?

All individuals are customers and every action that one chooses to do is a service. One's body language can also be conceived as customer service. It's not always what you say but sometimes it's what you do. For instance if someone cuts in front of you while you are driving, do you immediately flip them the bird? If a coworker or a boss asks you to do something for them during a busy time for you what is your body language saying? Your action can say yes while your body language says no. Do you frown and show negative facial expressions when you don't want to do something? As the saying goes actions speaks louder than words sometimes as it relates to service.

Going outside of the box doing homework is a service to yourself. If you shortchange the process you only cheat yourself out of an education. You can't cheat and skip your way through school and expect to land a job in a fortune 500 company. On the other hand if you are always at the top of your class you should expect to always be at the top of your company. Doing chores at home is a service to your household. Hopefully nobody wants to live in a dirty or nasty house. A great rule of thumb is if you help mess it up you should help clean it up. If you neglect to service or clean your house you are setting a bad example for your children, spouse, siblings, roommates, houseguest, visitors, etc. And not only that, but you unknowingly uninvited people, as nobody wants to hang around dirt, filth, and funk except unwanted critters and creatures.

Have you ever walked into a place and failed to open the door for the person walking directly behind you? For those who didn't know, holding a door is a service to the recipient. Now if you're in church, a concert, or a facility that is housing a lot of individuals you don't have to hold the door for everyone as this could take hours. But it is rude to allow a door to close on someone walking directly behind you. It is a way to hold the door just enough for the person behind you without closing it on them and they have the option to decide if they want to do the same. From another standpoint if you are walking into a building and you have someone walking in that may be handicapped, elderly, or just in need of assistance it is the proper thing to do. You never take your health, wholeness, and strength for granted as one day you could be in a wheel chair or need a walker. In this event you would definitely want someone to assist you with a door that you are unable to open yourself.

In this chapter we have learned that everything you do is a service. If you always give good service you should always expect good service. When you don't give good service you don't know what good service looks like. Service always begins at home and extends everywhere you go. Service is not always in big deeds but begins with small gestures. For instance at home cooking and cleaning for your family is a service. Washing clothes, washing dishes, cutting grass, washing a car, spending time with family, and the list goes on are all services. Your family will appreciate you more and be willing to return the favor when you service them.

Service should never be taken for granted and will only be extended to the extent you are willing to service. If you don't know that being mean is a disservice than you will think this is okay. You should never be allowed to partake in any position of leadership if you first do not know how to give service. You are toxic to the organization as you can't teach what you don't know. And the truth is most companies focus more on individual's credentials than that individual's ability to provide great service. Credentials will never triumph good service in the marketplace. Having a Dr's degree with poor customer service is equivalent to a high school dropout as it relates to life. The reason is simple because some individuals who have a title or position gain status that goes directly to their head. They become entitled and began to think they are better than others. Money, position, title, and status misused do not make you better than others but it openly displays ignorance as all men and women were created equal.

In no way am I discrediting those individuals highly educated, with high status, or at the top of the food chain. I'm just showing that they too have the responsibility of servicing but on a larger scale. For instance if you take Oprah Winfrey, she deserves to be treated royalty because of her status, accolades, accomplishments, and hard work. But on the other side she still has the same service responsibility as everyone else. She service's indirectly by thanking those who service her and directly by being kind to those in her circle as well as those that help and support her brand.

When you truly understand that everything you do is a service you will always be mindful of your choices. You never want to be remembered for a bad service experience especially when you had the opportunity to make the experience great. So for example let's say Shaquille O'Neal also known as Shaq is your favorite basketball player of all time. If you finally get the chance to meet Shaq and he does not care to engage with you it could be devastating.

Being more specific if you are in the grocery store and Shaq walks past you and you say Shaq, man it's an honor to meet you, I'm your biggest fan, and I'm currently attending LSU on a basketball scholarship because of you, etc. After you finish Shaq says ok great and walks off, your experience was very disappointing as Shaq failed to give you great service. But on the other side of this if Shaq says wow, what an honor. I'm so glad you followed in my footsteps and I wish you all the best. Then Shaq would say a joke something like "Young Fellow, you know I shoot better than Steph Curry, LOL." That's just what Shaq does, he jokes but this would definitely be a memorable experience. Not only did Shaq give the young man the wow factor but he serviced above and beyond. The young fellow would never forget this experience as it would only motivate him even more to go and be great. This example just shows that as a celebrity you have a fan base to service and a much greater service responsibility.

Since we tend to tie in service to dining let's look at servicing from a dining perspective that doesn't involve a direct line to customers. If a McDonald's worker comes in to work with a dirty uniform he does a disservice to himself, his peers, the customers, and most importantly the McDonalds brand. The impact of this poor service decision could cause a loss of business, a hostile work environment, low productivity, and the list goes on. First and foremost you lose business because nobody wants to eat where someone in a dirty uniform is making their food, servicing them, or in plain view sight. The environment becomes hostile because workers don't want to work with other employees who fail to clean their uniform as they began to exchange unpleasantries. The productivity goes down because the focus is on the worker with the dirty uniform versus the customers. So by making a decision to come to work with a dirty uniform the worker not only made himself look bad but his fellow employees as well as the McDonalds brand. You never know how big of an impact or affect that your decision to service directly or indirectly will affect those whom you come in contact with.

Service is not just in the big stuff but it's also in the littlest things as well. For instance giving customer's napkins is a service. It's a very small thing but that customer will leave disappointed if they go searching for a napkin only to realize you failed to give them some. Leaving utensils out of the bag can be a disservice to your guest as they may be going somewhere they don't have access to utensils and you failed to provide them with their meal. Telling your guest to have a good day along with greeting them is a form of service. Service is underrated and underappreciated but is a necessity.

Chapter 4 – To Give Is To Receive

Everyone should approach customer service using to give is to receive approach. This simply means that whatever you put out you receive in return. If this was the case in life how much differently will you treat others? If the answer is a lot than you may want to work on your service. However if the answer is not much differently this simply means that you are on the right track and to keep running the race. You can't treat people any kind of way and expect to be treated like a king or queen in return. This is a double standard as life does not work this way. Remember what you do in the dark will come to the light and what goes around comes around. Never give service that you would be ashamed of attaching to your name as your service represents you as an individual.

Since life is not a payback or repayment plan, you should never expect something in return for a good deed. You should want to service people out of the kindness of your heart and your reward is the joy they experience due to a great service experience. However if you give great service you should never be willing to receive anything less. You choose who you hang around, who you associate with, and who enters into your normal everyday service circle. If the individual's who are in your circle cannot service you than they need to not be in your circle. And since we already established that customer service cannot be confined to four walls you still have say so over your experiences and encounters. For instance you pick and choose what restaurants, grocery stores, gas stations, shopping malls, etc. that you will shop at. Some stores such as Chick Filet and Starbucks have great reputations for great service and will never lose the race because of this. Some stores have great reputations for being clean, neat, and organized like Target and Publix. Some stores have great reputations for convenience, quick and friendly service, and all purpose like QT and Wawa. On the other side you have some stores known for long lines, lack of workers, poor customer service, bad quality, etc. but we won't mention any names. The stores that fail to provide quality service are the stores that will fail to increase in revenue long term.

There are many surfaces and layers to service. Going back to the stores, customer service extends far beyond what you see (surface). Service with a smile, clean business, organized business, speedy service, well lit, greeters, clean rest rooms, properly staffed, quality products, clean uniforms, workers having a good time, friendly staff, and the list goes on to other avenues (layers) of service companies can provide. All service begins internally and filters over to the external. This basically means the service that is given within will filter to the outside. So if the management team does a poor job servicing its workers than the workers will do a poor job serving its guest. The general manager has a very critical role and must be service oriented. Too many times companies hire leadership based on lengthy resumes, accolades, educational accomplishments, and paper celebrations. While these items are all important the single most important thing does not exist when searching for a leader. The number one quality every company should search for in a leader (CEO) or leadership position is customer service. Just because you meet the qualifications does not mean you know how to service the guests. If you eliminate customer service from leadership you eliminate revenue from your bottom line. If you leader who may not even touch the guest cannot service his employees than you have done yourself a disservice as a company. We will talk more about customer service as it relates to business in the very next chapter.

To give is to receive is a life principle that you can apply and plug into many different scenarios. So let's take school for instance, have you ever had a big test that you had to take? I talking about an exam, end of school year test, test to see if you go to the next grade, get the promotion test, internship test, military entry test, etc. I'm talking about SAT, ACT, ASVAB, GED test or just larger than life kind of test. Those types of tests take a lot out of you as they require a lot of investment, strategy, and personal time. This same principle is what you apply to your time spent preparing for this test. If you give time, excessive effort, extra practice, extra review time, etc. then you will receive a passing grade. Because of what you were willing to invest you were able to reap a great investment.

This same scenario holds true for customer service as you get what you give. If you always give stellar service you will always receive stellar service. Does this mean everyone will always give you superb service? Absolutely, positively not as this will not always be the desired case simply because you can't control people and not everyone is customer oriented. But because you give service at such a high level you would not be willing to receive service at a lower level. Simply stating you won't stick around for anything less than what you are giving as this becomes the standard. The better you give great service the more you began to know what great service looks like both near and far.

An example of giving and receiving is found in every day routines such as receiving mail from your local post office. As the customer you can give the postal carrier good service by emptying your mailbox frequently, ensuring you have a clean and secure mailbox, never block your mailbox, never give your pet direct access to your mail handler, and cut or trim all bushes that surround your mailbox. Your mail handler should not have to fight to put stuff in the box because you are too lazy to empty your box. Your mailbox should be secure meaning it does not fall apart when you open it or even fall to the ground. It is very disrespectful and inconvenient when you block your mailbox regularly or intentionally as it tells your mail handler you don't want any mail. If you have a dog or another animal please don't allow them to jump on or harass your mail carrier as not everyone is pet friendly. They may not bite you but you never know what they may do to someone else. And your mail carrier should be able to access your mailbox without having to fight off bushes, weeds, and trees.

As a mail carrier you service your customer by not stuffing packages or mail in the box. If it doesn't fit take it to the door or back to the post office as directed. As a mail carrier you should not damage anyone's mailbox, shortchange them on their mail, throw their packages, open anyone's mail, or anything of that sort. You treat the customer the same way you want someone to treat you when they deliver your mail. So as you see it is a give and receive. If you give your mail carrier good service they will return the favor and vice versa as this is how it should be.

Let's look at another example, so say you stop by a convenient store for a snack. You have $1 and decide to purchase a fifty cents honey bun with no taxes included. You give the sales clerk your one dollar bill and in return the clerk provides you with the fifty cents honey bun and fifty cents in change. You gave one dollar and you received fifty cents along with a fifty cent honey bun. This is just another example of how to give is to receive works. Anything you purchase you will receive along with a balance if there is anything left over upon payment as it relates to giving and receiving service.

When you are talking service there is always something given as well as something being received. You cannot have a service transaction without an exchange. The ultimate goal is to have a great smooth exchange process with both sides leaving filling accomplished. If both individuals do not get serviced than it's not an equal exchange. Going back to the honey bun scenario if the customer only provided forty five cents, this is not an equal exchange. And on the other side if the clerk only gives the customer back forty five cents this is not an equal exchange. If one side gets cheated it's a good chance they will no longer do business together anymore. When you feel like you are not being serviced to satisfaction than you will begin to go elsewhere for service.

If you are the giver or on the giving end of a service encounter, you should always want to give your best. Let's just say you had a business and you are giving out free samples of a new product. Because it's free would you cheat the customer out of the product or would you give them the same product you plan to sell? Hopefully you are giving the customer the product that you plan to sell. Just because you are giving it out free does not mean that you short change the service process. You should still want to exceed the customers' expectations as your today in the service industry will usually determine your tomorrow's success. If you go the extra mile with your free samples than you leave the customer with a memorable experience. Not only will they call their peers and say come and get some free samples but they will return as long as the product matches the experience.

On the other side of this if you cheat the consumer out of product or the process they will tell everyone and post it on social media. And you're giving experience will turn into a nightmare as you will lose business instead of gaining business all because you cheated your customers out of a service experience. If you are giving for anything but out of the kindness of your heart you should not give. You should never give with expectations to receive something in return. The reason you don't put expectations on giving is because if your expectations are not met you will be disappointed with the outcome.

If you are a receiver you should always desire to receive the best. Never have low expectancy on what you are entitled to receive. If you pay for a service you are entitled to receive that service. For example if you pay someone to cut your grass you should not be okay with mediocre service. This simply means that if you paid someone to cut your grass than you should not have part of your grass cut but your entire yard should have been serviced. The trimming, cutting hedges, and manicure may cost you more as you should always get at the least what you paid for. If you are okay with receiving any kind of service you may be okay with giving any kind of service.

If we go back to the business giving out the free product than as a receiver you want to receive the best. What if it was free food that the company was giving out? As a receiver if the food was no good you would not return and probably warn others. However if the food was excellent you would probably return as a paying customer and call some others to join you. When it comes to receiving you should always expect to receive the best. You should always value yourself enough to know that you are entitled to the best as it relates to receiving service.

When you understand the importance of to give is to receive as it relates to service you will never sell yourself short from the giving or the receiving end. Whether it's a purchase from a store or a gift exchange with friends you will always give the best and expect the best. Now with this being said if you are doing a work gift exchange and the budget is five dollars per gift you should get the best five dollar gift money can buy whether it be a gift card or specific item. If you spend two dollars for a gift exchange gift with a five dollar budget you should not expect your gift to be a five dollar gift. If the item the individual wants is only two dollars than use the other three dollars to purchase a second gift. To give is to receive is customer service at its best.

Chapter 5 – Customer Service & How It Relates to Business

Customer service and business goes together just as a husband and wife. A business in today's society does not exist without customer service. Show me a thriving business and I'll show you extravagant customer service. Show me a poor performing business and I'll show you no or bare minimum customer service. Technology does not exclude a company from participating in the ultimate customer service experience. The more technical the company is the greater the service experience should be.

Not only is it up to employees to provide customer service but it's time for employers to do the same. This is not the norm for **most** businesses but success within also relies heavily on in house customer service. You cannot expect your employees to do this if you as an employer are not willing to do the same. When it comes to customer service the standard cannot be a do as I say standard but it must be a do as I do, led by example. If you treat your employees good, than they will know how to treat your customers good. However if you treat your employees bad you cannot seriously expect them to treat your customers stellar.

Some may ask how do you provide customer service to your employees? Glad you asked as there are many ways you can provide customer service to your employees. For one you deliver on any and every promise you make to that employee. Don't tell them you are going to give them a raise if you can't afford to do it. You talk to them with respect and never down talk your employees because they are lower ranking. Remember they are people just like you, God created everyone as equals meaning don't let a title go to your head.

An employee will leave you faster for lying or mistreatment than they will money. You take care of the employees just as you would your very own children or spouse. They may not get the same treatment but it shouldn't be too far off. Remember this is your business and you are relying on your workers to come thru for you. You can't expect someone to take ownership or have pride in the workplace if you don't empower them to do so as an employer. You should trust your employees to do the job that you hired them to do. Trust goes a long way and can take ones confidence to the moon and back. It's simple, if you don't trust someone don't hire them.

Don't punish your team members for one employee failing to deliver. You invest or pour into your employees as this investment will one day yield a return. The return is based on what you were willing to invest into them. You can't expect to produce a CEO when you only invested into a junior cashier status. For example if you invest $50 into a stock, bond, bank account, etc. you can't expect a $500,000 investment return without waiting an eternity as this is unrealistic. You should always train your employees for the next level and those who show increased potential you invest more.

Going back to Chapter 3 we discussed how employers should never employ leaders who lack great customer service. In fact there should be a customer service survey established for all leadership roles. The higher the position the more detailed the survey should be. Ask yourself are you ok with hiring a Chief Executive Officer (CEO) who you will pay 100k salary who lacks the ability to provide great customer service? If a leader lacks great customer service how can they truly know what it looks like or if it's missing within their company?

Too many times we tend to focus more on the person who will lead than the service they will be able to provide. While it's great to have the credentials and a fancy resume, if they lack basic customer service fundamentals than you are truly losing as a company. Are you prepared to shape the face of your company with a noncustomer eccentric leader? As an employer or leader never be that boss or business that you demand excellent customer service from your employees but don't give the same in return. If you are presently in leadership and lack great customer service you should look at how this is affecting your business. Even if your bottom line is presently bringing in revenue, look at how much you are leaving on the table.

The ultimate goal of any business is to be profitable. The way a company becomes profitable is by serving its customers. You as a leader have to take the necessary steps to become better in providing stellar customer service. What's on the head will most definitely flow down to the tail. As a leader in your industry you set the tone and tender for your company. Never forget the seeds you sow are the seeds you grow. This simply means that whatever you invest in (your vision) is where your company focus will grow in. You should never be willing to grow your company in an area that won't sustain your company's operational longevity.

Since there is so much competition in the marketplace in today's society there should be more urgency as it relates to customer service. For example you rarely see a business that does not have a competitor within its direct peripheral. For instance when you see a McDonalds you usually see a Burger King, Hardees, Taco Bell, Jack n the Box, or other fast food establishment. When you see KFC you usually see Bojangles', Popeye's, Churches, Golden Skillet, etc. When you see a State farm Insurance agent you typically see a Nationwide, Progressive, Geico, etc. When you see a Walmart you typically see a Target, Food Lion, Ukrops, Farm Fresh, Kroger, etc. When you see an IHOP you see a Waffle House, Crackle Barrel, etc. When you see Walgreens you see an Eckerd Drug, Rite Aide, CVS Pharmacy, etc. When you see a Mercedes dealership you see a Cadillac dealership,

Bentley dealership, Infiniti dealership, BMW dealership, Tesla dealership, etc.

The point is for every business exist direct competition and if they are not located directly across then they are on the way. You rarely see just one gas station within a certain mile radius. With this being said what separates your business from the next? Why would someone choose your business over your competition? What can you offer that your competition will not? Why will your customers choose you consistently? How can you raise the bar in sales and consistently have quarterly sales gains? What will you do differently to keep your business growing in such a competitive market place? What will keep your doors from closing?

Every answer to these questions can all be answered with great customer service. People want to go where they are treated the best and receive the greatest service. Competitive prices can also play a big role in a company's sustainability but customer service is always key. The three things that keep's a company relevant are customer service, pricing, and products or services offered. Customer service is the single most and biggest reason for a company's long-term success. Pricing is good but bad service and good pricing will eventually push people away and business will die down slowly or only appeal to the lower class. Great products and bad service will have the same effect as it will eventually push people away slowly. Nobody wants to spend hard earned money somewhere they don't feel appreciated as it's too much competition to settle.

Now if we answer the questions above it would look something like this. Customer service separates your business from the next. This is simple because customer service is the one thing you can offer that you can either beat out or fall short as it relates to your local competition. Customer service is why someone would choose your business over your competition. If you are always smiling, welcoming, accommodating, and friendly this can be a game changer and draw customers to you versus your competitor. You can offer superb customer service and beat out your competition. If your competition is only greeting there guest you can go the extra mile by greeting, checking on them while they are in your business, and giving an exit greeting.

Your customers will choose you consistently because of your customer service. Customers want to feel valued, appreciated, be acknowledged, be respected, and be accommodated. You can raise the bar in sales and consistently have a quarterly sales gain by gradually increasing your customer service. The greater the service you provide the more customers you attract which in turn increases your bottom line. When people receive great service they tend to spread the word as word of mouth can be good or bad publicity depending on the service you provide. Getting creative in customer service approaches is a way to keep your business growing in such a competitive market place.

Let's look at Chick Filet, they have workers outside in all weather conditions in the drive thru to help during their busiest breakfast, lunch, or dinner rushes to expedite the service. This not only wows the guest because they are getting great service but it makes them feel special that someone would take the time just for them to ensure their experience is great. Creative customer service sometimes involves going outside the box but you should always be willing to change your approach based on customer's wants and needs as you want to be where they are.

Customer service will keep your doors from closing. If you have the best customer service in your industry people will always want to come to you first. Toys R' US, one of the largest toy retailers in the US has closed its doors. It came as a shock as there are not many large toy only retailers in the US. While they had one of the best children's toys selections, there customer service was never a major discussion at any point in time. Now they are looking to reestablish themselves presently by reopening stores worldwide but only time will tell if they will invest in providing the best customer service ever.

Nonprofits also have the same responsibility as it relates to customer service. Some examples include but are not limited to American Red Cross, Habitat for Humanity, The Salvation Army, Goodwill Industries, Better Business Bureau, and churches worldwide. Now if we take Goodwill Industries as an example, Reverend Edgar J Helms was the founder in 1902. When Goodwill was established it was created to help and provide aid for all individuals. There reputation at that time was all about the customer as they went above and beyond. Presently can you say that customers run to goodwill because they believe they will receive this same level of service or is it for a bargain? If your company has a reputation for helping people as most nonprofits do the customer service has to be superb. You never stray away from your success as a company you just find ways to enhance what's already working. It's all about building a brand that all starts with the customer whether it's for profit or a nonprofit establishment.

There is no substitute for great customer service in the marketplace. If your company is struggling you should start with your customer service and then begin to work on everything else that may need to be adjusted. Too many times businesses take customer service for granted when in actuality it is the secret sauce to keeping their business in the green. Why should a customer shop with you when you have x amount of competitors within x amount of feet?

You really have to ask yourself this question and then answer it honestly. If your employees are not customer oriented please do not put them on the front line or anywhere that they are in direct contact with customers. If you are a business that deals with vendors please understand that these vendors are your customers as you work together for the greater good. Stop thinking they owe you something or you owe them something. It's a customer service business relationship as you owe it to each other as a service partnership where you take care of each other. If the truth be told you need each other to survive even though we often think otherwise.

Never ever think that technology and innovation will replace customer service. The truth is the more technology you have the more customer service you need. For instance a lot of grocery stores have self check out. While this can sometimes be fast, quick, and convenient it's not always a great experience. And advancement will never replace great service no matter how much technology evolves. A successful business is one that puts the customer first and truly invests in customer service starting with the top leadership all the way down to the bottom. A company with a leader in place who has poor customer service skills is like a business without a vision, without a mission, and without goals.

Some other key factors from a business standpoint may consist of offering benefits for your employees and their entire family. If you can't provide for the entire family it tells the single employee your valuable and the employee with the family that your family's not that important. Having accessibility for handicapped individuals to enter and exit your business as well as vendors. Just because someone has a disability or handicap does not make them less important. And how can vendors bring in product if your store is not vendor friendly?

Sharing your bonus with your team that helped you to earn this extra compensation whether directly or indirectly should always be the norm. You didn't earn it by yourself and should not spend it all by yourself even if you just have a party for the team and feed them as this shows your appreciation. And never surprise your employees on their paycheck when there is bad news. Unfortunately a great amount of our society lives paycheck to paycheck as one unexpected interruption can be the difference in someone being homeless.

This customer service tip will not get a lot of likes but it is so timely in today's society, get your mouth off your leader for employees and get your mouth off your employees for your leader. Gossiping is not customer service, never has been, and should not be tolerated in the workplace as you have to cut it off at the root. Get your mouth off your company that you willingly represent because whether you like it or not you accepted the position and don't have to work there. Follow the chain of command and stay within the order of operations. When you break the order you are violating company policy and disrespecting the service flow that's been established within the company. Please answer the phones professionally and with integrity at all times because you never know who's on the other end. The phone should never be off the hook and never ring more than three times as you are running a business.

Other key customer service pointers are no stealing from work even if you are feeding your family it's not your food and you did not pay for it, it's not your supplies and you did not pay for it. Too many times workers whether it be employees, management, or employers believe they are entitled to company property due to lack of pay, work provided, or just outright entitlement. If you did not pay for the merchandise it is not yours and you are stealing. Having a restroom with soap to wash your hands that is in full operation for your guest is a no brainer when it comes to customer service. How can you have an establishment where customers are coming and spending there hard earned money and you don't have a public restroom for them? Or you have a restroom but you don't have any soap or toilet paper. Not having soap or even toilet paper is a disrespectful disservice to your guest. This goes back to treating people how you want to be treated. If you have it in your house for yourself it should be in your business for your guest.

One of the most important factors for customer service as it relates to business is having integrity.

Building a relationship to up sell a guest based on needs versus commission is integral. If you wear the I get paid by commission hat you can't expect customers to do anything other than say I'm just looking to run you off and buy some time. This just means I want to be left alone because your approach is not genuine and you really don't care about me but about the money I spend. Having integrity can be as simple as being on time, being honest, performing required work, paying employees for all of their hours versus rounding time up or down as this is illegal and unethical, and working honorably from home, etc. When you clock in are you ready to work or do you clock in and go to the restroom or break room? So many times you see employees stealing time on all levels just because they can. When you are on salary are you working your required hours or do you come a little late because nobody is watching?

When your employer asks you to park in the back so the customers can park in the front, do you comply with their request? Do you clean up after yourself in the work place when you make a mess? Or do you leave it for maintenance or the custodian to clean? For attorneys do you fully service every client you represent or do you just see them as a source to your paycheck? For a judge do you give service to criminals or innocent individuals on trial for crimes they did not commit or do you see yourself as better than them because of your title? For the President do you service everyone or just particular groups because you have the greatest title? For the car dealers and mechanics are you integral with your practices or are your customers being ripped off? For the government do you hold everyday citizens to the laws and allow government officials to slide because of their titles? Should the president be required to do his taxes and report his finances with integrity if everyone else has to? Customer service is not racial, prejudice, opinioned, one-sided, gender favored, bipolar, schizophrenic, or self-centered.

Customer service as it relates to business has so many layers but it all starts with leadership. What are you willing to do to ensure your company provides the best quality of service? And most importantly how do you sustain this service over time? As time and innovation changes you have to be willing to change your service strategy. Just because you send out packages does not mean that you are excluded. Did you go the extra mile and put a thank you card in the box for their purchase? Do you pay your workers a respectable wage that matches their required job description? Remember when you don't invest in customer service as it relates to your business you shorten your companies lifespan as it's only a matter of time before your competitor takes your customers. Ask yourself are you willing to be the company that is cutting edge, strategic, and innovative when it comes to customer service?

Chapter 6 – Customer Service at Home

Customer service truly starts at home before it can be taken to the market place or outside world. Since we already established that customer service is a life thing and it's everywhere you go now we must know where our execution comes from. Our first example of customer service comes from our parents or guardian. Growing up your outlook is limited to what you see as this doesn't mean it won't expand pass this but the chances are very slim. If you see your parents, guardians, older siblings, etc. respecting one another than you would tend to do the same.

Since this is your first example of customer service it is very critical that it's a positive experience. However if you see the exact opposite such as disrespect, swearing, violence, etc. taking place than you are already at a disadvantage as it relates to customer service. You are what you eat which simply means you become whatever is deposited in you. Again this doesn't mean you can't change your outlook but it's very rare that this change occurs. If you only see bad than you only know bad and your mind will begin to think this is just how life is.

From a parents perspective it is very critical that you service your children even if you weren't serviced as a child. You now have the chance to rewrite any wrongs that you experienced as a child. First and foremost you never argue or fight in front of your child or children. Always do this quietly behind closed doors and if it cannot be resolved than split up until things cool down as violence whether verbal or physical is never healthy for a child at any point in time. Never allow yourself or your children to limit their life to their surroundings. For instance if you live in the projects, don't say it's always gone be like this as your words have power. Don't expect your future generations to be raised in the same projects.

Instead start preparing them for better by speaking to your situation, investing in education, refusing to no longer settle, and most importantly change your surroundings. If you want to be something bigger you have to hang around something bigger. You cannot hang around drug dealers, gang bangers, killers, pot heads, addicts, prostitutes, etc. and expect to do something different. You will become them or they will become you as it's usually easier to become them because the fight for them to become you takes much more than natural normalcy.

You service your children by the way you speak to them. Saying no ma'am, yes ma'am to a child at a young age does wonders as it makes them feel important. Too many times you hear people say don't call me ma'am or sir, I work for a living especially in the military. When actuality is this is a simply a sign of respect as you don't want your children calling you or any other adult by their first name. Saying ma'am and sir has nothing to do with your employer or working it's simply a way of showing respect. Yes or no sounds way better than what or huh as it relates to your child or children's response. You also service your people by the example you set for your children.

As a father who has a daughter you are the first example of a man they will see. Every father should date his daughter first. What does this mean; it simply means you treat your daughter like the princess that she is. You want her experience with a man to be all that and a bag of chips. You open the doors for your daughter, you kiss her boo boos, you play with her on her terms even if it is doll babies, you hold her hand, you read her a story at night time, you tuck her into bed every night, you kiss and hug her excessively, you provide for her, and you are always there for her when she needs you. If you do this when it's her time to start dating she will accept no less as this is always a tough transition for real father's, the letting go process but it will make it easier knowing she's in good hands.

Any father who has a son should be a true example of what a gentleman looks like. A gentleman is someone who is chivalrous, courteous, or honorable. If your son sees these qualities in you and this is all he knows that he in turn will desire to become the same. Your son should see you respecting women, opening doors, providing for his family, being an amazing husband, being an amazing friend, honoring mom and dad, being a respectable leader, loving, law abiding citizen, and living an all around enjoyable life. As a man you should teach your son how to be a respectable family man and effectively reproduce a family of his own. If you are violent with words or physically you tell your son this is okay. If you neglect your family and responsibility you tell your son this is okay. You are the first example of what a man is suppose to look like.

As a mother you should teach your son what a real help mate looks like. If you are married your son should see you as having dads back and working as a team. The traditional family looks like dad going to work and mom running the household. If this is the case your son should see the best version of this. However in today's society you have a lot of working moms as well as single moms. If you are a working mom your son should still see positive interaction between you and dad and what teamwork looks like. If your son sees division, down talk, and disruption they will think this is the norm. As a single parent show your son what hard work looks like and be the example of what a real woman looks like. And even if the father is not present never down talk his dad or deny access as this will go along way when he gets older. While a woman cannot raise a boy to be a man she can exemplify a strong woman.

As a mother you want to teach your daughter how to be an amazing woman. You set the standard by teaching them to take pride in themselves by always investing in their outward as well as their inward appearance. Most importantly teach your daughter how to run and maintain their household. Teach them to be independent as well as a team player. A woman should never be solely dependent on a man as this will only set them up for failure if they think they can't survive without a man. A mother should always teach their daughters order, cleanliness, and consistency.

As a sibling to a brother or sister it is your responsibility to exchange customer service with each other from day to day. You service your sibling by helping them, encouraging, protecting them, and watching them. If you are the oldest you have the greatest responsibility to look out for your brother or sister. Your younger sibling watches you and looks up to you so you have to be careful what example you set for them. You always treat your sibling with respect and honor as they are connected to you for life. Siblings will fight or have disagreements as this is a part of life but apologizing and forgiving one another is a part of the service process. When you make a mistake being quick to acknowledge and ask for their forgiveness is how you truly show them they are important to you.

Married folks should service one another in deeds, gifts, words, and commitments. When you said I do, you took vows to honor, respect, cherish, and love one another till death do you part. This day and age we don't take these vows serious all the time as we often give up way too easy. But how you live up to these vows is how you service your spouse. You should also service one another in the bedroom as there should be no shortage of love expressions. And since nobody's perfect there will be arguments or disagreements as this is a way to service one another too. The way you give customer service to your spouse doing a fiery moment is to not respond or simply put just shut up. Two people cannot argue when one chooses not to participate as this diffuses the fire and prevents an exchange of nasty words or tit for tat. In marriage there are many sacrifices that are made daily as this is how you service your mate. An example if you like steak and she likes seafood you put your desires to the side to satisfy her wants. In return she will desire to want to please you because of your willingness to sacrifice for her. Laughter is a much needed service that will get you through both good and bad times. Never forget that marriage is a partnership, the more you are willing to service your spouse the more they will want to service you.

Customer service is vital in your home as you will only get out what you put in as it relates to your household. You can't expect to get something you are not willing to give. And as a parent or guardian it is vital that you not only service but sacrifice for the sake of your children. Whatever you deposit into your children or household will yield a return in the same form. Be mindful of your investment yielding a return, for instance if you sow love into your household you will reap love. But if you sow hatred and malice you will receive the same in return. Always be willing to make time for friends, family and coworkers. Never get to the place where you are too busy to enjoy life.

You should never expect or demand service from family when you are not willing to yield the same. Whether you are a parent or the head of your household you still owe it to your children or spouse to service them. A greater title or being the bread winner does not exclude you from the process. If anything you have a bigger responsibility to service your love ones with a greater title. As stated before we were all created equal and nobody is excluded from customer service.

Customer Service "It's A Life Thing"

Chapter 7 – Customer Service at Its Best

Customer Service at its best is when you generally care about servicing another individual with no motive or hidden agenda involved. There should be a goal in mind as it relates to customer service whether it is business or personnel. For instance if you are a company your goal is for the customer to come back. If you are a husband or wife your goal is to honor your commitment and exceed your spouse's expectations. If you are a parent your goal is to be the most loving, generous, honorable, and exciting parent you can be. It should be your goal to make every service encounter a pleasant one. And in the event you fall short dust yourself off and learn from it so you can do better next time around.

Building relationships is key and a critical piece to executing customer service whether it is business or personal. Try finding out at least one personnel thing you did not know about your customer before. Other things you can do is offer assistance before they ask, predetermine their needs, ask for their name, go out of your way to extend assistance, make time in your schedule for someone else, give a just because gift, allow someone else to go ahead of you, and be a good listener to someone in need. Stop looking to always be the recipient on the receiving end of great customer service and challenge yourself to be a leader or change agent for service.

Always put yourself in the equation when you think of customer service. What would I want? How would I like to be treated? What would I expect? How would I react? What would I do? What would I like to receive? How would I love? How would I give? How would I make the proposal? How would I rewrite a wrong? Always be willing to give what you expect to receive in return. As my Apostle, Dr. Travis Jennings would say, "Take the stairs because the elevator is out of service." That simply says there is no shortcut to great customer service. The sooner you realize this the sooner you are able to experience and enjoy the entire ride. If you shortchange the process you shortchange the experience and results meaning you just eliminated the wow factor from the encounter.

Some desired results you can expect to see from customer service at is best is smiles, handshakes, hugs, kisses, high fives, head nods, love letters, marriage proposals, repeat business, customers for life, trustworthy friendships, truthful family members, extravagant children, productive parents, respectable individuals, integral individuals, caring individuals, diligent leaders, successful leaders, honest leaders, open leaders, successful business transactions, increase of customers, lucrative business deals, new opportunities, expansion, top notch employees, increased profit margins, longevity, and the list goes on. When customer service is at its best you have a contagious environment that everyone wants to be a part of. It's time for the leaders, influencers, and global movers to infect the world with extraordinary service so much that it spreads like a wildflower throughout the globe.

To ensure your customer service is at its best you have to correct some wrongs. You should avoid approaching men or women that have on wedding rings as they cannot help you achieve your own personal needs. If they have on a ring it clearly says they are married, getting married, or just unavailable. You should avoid texting at the dinner table or during meaningful family events as this should be valuable time you spend with your family, love ones or friends. Cell phones should never take precedence over family time and must be turned off during certain times. Turning off or putting away your cell phone at certain specific times simply says you're important to me, I value your time, you have my undivided attention, I honor our time together, etc.

Some things that keep you from having your best service experience is popping bubble gum in a professional environment, allowing your dog to use the bathroom in someone else's yard, not keeping yourself well groomed, not watching your kids in public places, making a mess in someone's establishment that you don't care to clean up, making dishes that you don't plan to wash, washing clothes that you don't care to fold, leaving a drop of kool aid or other beverage in the refrigerator, leaving the toilet seat up when you have females in your house, cutting on all the lights in the house when you don't contribute to the light bill, being an inconvenience by asking someone with a family to stay at their home, standing on the street corner with a sign begging for food, wearing provocative clothing in the public that disrespects you and your heritage without proper covering, wearing clothes too big and too small, and the list goes on.

Customer service is at its best when you are at your best. You cannot give amazing service when you are less than your best. If you are unable to provide the full experience it is best that you wait until you are feeling better. It is impossible to please someone else when you can't please yourself. You have to be happy and comfortable with who you are before you are able to provide the best service ever. If you are always sincere and intentional with your service than your service will always come out the same consistently. Every time you interact and service an individual it is a reflection of who you truly are. While you can put on an act and fool some people just remember that this will soon wear off and the real you will be revealed in time. If you are not happy with your service it's time to make a change. Remember, you control the delivery of your service.

The key to amazing service is remembering that customer service takes place everywhere individuals are. For instance a teacher services their students by doing what they say they will do. If a teacher says they will give out grades every Friday they service the students by maintaining this standard that they set. On the other side of this a student services their teacher by being quiet while the lesson is going on, being attentive, not being disruptive, listening, following directions, not listening to music, not being on their cell phones during class, and raising their hand to talk. When both sides service one another it's a win, win as the focus for the teacher is to teach and the focus for the student is to learn. Customer service at its best is when everyone is in unison on one accord working together to achieve desired results.

As a doctor you can perform great customer service by treating each patient as if they are one of your loved ones, keeping your office clean, ensuring the patient understands what you are saying, take the time to invest in your patient, and be friendly. If you had to perform surgery on your mother, father, spouse, child, etc. how would you prepare or treat your patient? What extra steps or measures would you take? Those same patients that you are servicing are hopeful of returning home to their love ones in the near future. And as a patient you can give great customer service by **listening** to your doctor. Listening can keep you out of the surgery room and even save your life in certain situations. Love your family enough (this is also how you service your family indirectly) by listening to the doctor to extend your lifeline. This just shows that nobody is excluded. Judges, lawyers, social workers, parole officers, police officers, professional athletes, broadcasters, photographers, journalists, engineers, body guards, millionaires, billionaires, etc. all share the same obligation to provide great customer service while performing your jobs daily with integrity.

Customer service is not always presented properly or considered to be right as this just means you have an opportunity to rewrite your wrongs. They say the customer is always right but this is not always true. Sometimes customers make mistakes as everyone has off -days, just remember everyone is a customer. Now customer service at its best is when you make the mistake and then intentionally apologize for being wrong without being told to do so. A sincere and genuine apology along with a deed will reestablish a broken relationship with time in most cases. For instance if you lie to a spouse, a parent, a child, a friend, a coworker, a supervisor, etc. this is far from customer service. You have an opportunity to make it right by sincerely apologizing and making a commitment to do better. Now on the other end of that you may have lost trust so you have to regain it by deeds, by showing with examples, by letting time pass, and etc. They may not want anything else to do with you but by telling the truth you just serviced yourself as well as the individual and they will respect you more in the long run. With this being said if you are consistent with lying or providing disservice to your guest they will be consistent in separating themselves from you as not every service experience has a happy ending.

Now that you understand that customer service is truly a life thing and it affects everything you do, how will you choose to live your life going forward? You probably never knew that customer service was so essential to today's society. Not only is it critical but its key to our freedom, peace, and mere existence today more than ever. If we were not willing to service other countries and make peace what do you think would be the outcome? Sure we got our challenges but without customer service everyday there is a war that exists where peace is nonexistent. And now that you know how important customer service is, it's up to you to ensure you not only execute but you educate others on the importance. I hope this has changed your perspective on how you view people and individuals going forward. Everyone is different as nobody was created the same. Many have different backgrounds and different upbringings but it does not make anyone less qualified to receive great service. When you embrace customer service and see it for the beauty that it is it will blossom and bloom throughout your life. Stop talking about change and let's go out and be the change that we desire.

Final Thoughts

I hope this book has enlightened you and have given you a true understanding of the importance of customer service. When we stop taking the little things for granted in life the bigger things will mean so much more. Customer service should never be an inconvenience or an interruption of your day but the beginning of your journey. This book was not written to offend anyone but to open eyes and challenge everyone. You can't fix what you don't know just as you can't change the past. However you can start from today forward by being the change you desire. You can't control others actions but you can control your actions. Followers are looking for leaders in today's world. Be the change, the direction, and the example that the world needs to see. No more waiting, for customer service starts with you and me.

Today's world is in desperate need of compassion, love, dedication, commitment, teamwork, unity, integrity, loyalty, passion, and peace. These are all components or building blocks of great customer service. The future existence of our world depends on today's decisions. Future generations are eagerly awaiting your responses. Will they rejoice in forgiveness or cease to exist in retaliation? Live your life in love and let your legacy reflect greatness through your works and deeds. Never let opportunity pass you by for we now know without any doubt, Customer Service, **It's A Life Thing!**

Customer Service "It's A Life Thing"

Luther T. Collins

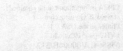

CPSIA information can be obtained
at www.ICGtesting.com
Printed in the USA
LVHW030510200620
658564LV00004B/312

9 780976 417705